GUITAR *Listen & Learn*
HOMESPUN MUSIC INSTRUCTION

Happy
TRAUM
TEACHES
Blues Guitar

A Hands-on Beginner's Course
in Acoustic Country Blues
*Featuring a Comprehensive
Audio Lesson on CD*

T0040915

Cover Photo by Dion Ogust

Audio Editor: George James

Mastered by: Ted Orr at
Nevessa Productions, Woodstock, N.Y.

ISBN 0-7935-6255-4

HOMESPUN®
Tapes

EXCLUSIVELY DISTRIBUTED BY
HAL•LEONARD®
7777 W. BLUEMOUND RD. P.O. BOX 13819 MILWAUKEE, WI 53213

© 1996 HOMESPUN TAPES LTD.
BOX 694
WOODSTOCK, NY 12498-0694
All Rights Reserved

CD instruction makes it easy! Find the section of the lesson you want with the press of a finger; play that segment over and over until you've mastered it; easily skip over parts you've already mastered—no clumsy rewinding or fast-forwarding to find your spot; listen with the best possible audio fidelity; follow along track-by-track with the book.

Table of Contents

PAGE	CD TRACK	
4	1	Introduction
	2	Tuning
	3	12-Bar Blues Explanation
5	4	12-Bar Blues, in E
		"Good Mornin' Blues"
	5	Introduction
6	6	"Good Mornin' Blues" Verses 1, 2&3
7	7	Turnarounds & Endings
8	8	Double-Stop Turnaround
8	9	Fills
10	10	"Good Mornin' Blues" with Fills, Verses 4&5
	11	Right Hand Rhythm
12	12	Rocking Bass Rhythms
	13	"Good Mornin' Blues" with Rocking Bass
13	14	Boogie Woogie Walking Bass
14	15	Bass Turnarounds
14	16	Happy's Favorite Turnaround
		"New Stranger Blues"
	17	Introduction
15	18	"New Stranger Blues"
18	19	Fingerstyle Blues, Breaking Up the Chords
19	20	Brownie's Lick
	21	"Good Mornin' Blues" with Brownie's Lick

PAGE	CD TRACK	
		"Rock Me Mama"
20	22	"Rock Me Mama"
	23	Breakdown & Analysis
	24	Slow Version
	25	More Breakdown & Analysis
22	25	Octave Variations
		"In the Evening When the Sun Goes Down"
	26	Introduction
23	27	"In the Evening When the Sun Goes Down
	28	Wrap-up
	29	"Kansas City Blues"
28		Chord Diagrams
29		Biography
30		A Selected Discography

This book contains music examples and all of the instructional songs from the CD, and are labeled with track icons (◆) for the ease of locating the corresponding tracks. The remaining tracks listed here contain detailed explanation and instruction for these songs.

Introduction

Fingerstyle acoustic blues guitar has been my favorite style since I started playing more than forty years ago. I originally learned by listening to records and playing with friends, but I also had a chance to take lessons directly from the great blues guitarist Brownie McGhee. Brownie's teaching method consisted of playing songs and guitar solos over and over while I picked along behind him, trying to keep up, making mistakes, playing hour after hour and finally developing a solidity and understanding of blues guitar that I never would have achieved through a more conventional system. Brownie was always patient and accommodating, and his generous example has remained with me through the years.

This lesson is for beginners in the blues style. I have tried to convey, through both the printed and recorded material in this package, the fun and satisfaction in playing this music. I have chosen the key of E as a starting point to give you a good, solid base to work with. It is also the most popular key for playing the blues with its open E and A strings. In later volumes, I will tackle other keys, but if you get this one down, it will take you a long way.

Fingerstyle playing in itself is a challenge, and I hope you can develop the necessary "independent thumb" whose job it is to keep the rhythm going, much like the left hand on a piano. Don't worry if you don't get it right away. This takes a good deal of practice and experience, and eventually you will get the hang of it.

I was lucky enough to have come up in a time when it was possible to see many of the great blues players in person—Brownie McGhee and Sonny Terry, Mississippi John Hurt, Skip James, Big Bill Broonzy, Rev. Gary Davis, Josh White and others—and I watched and absorbed as much as I could during the years they were around. Nowadays there has been a resurgence of interest in this guitar style, and there is a new generation of players carrying on the tradition and creating a new one for the future. I hope you will listen to as many of these as you can, and go back to the recordings of the original blues greats as well. Between them, you'll surely find the inspiration to blaze your own trails in this uniquely American musical form.

Happy Traum

◆4 12-Bar Blues
(in E)

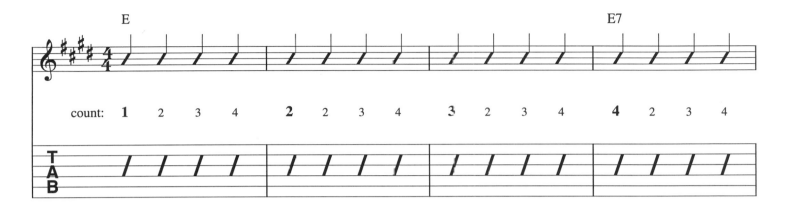

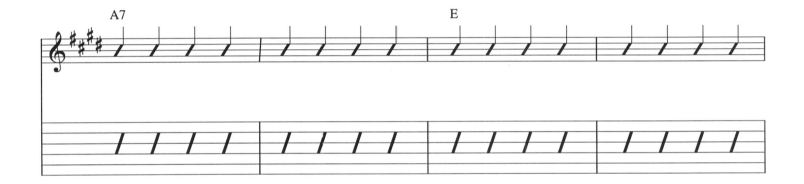

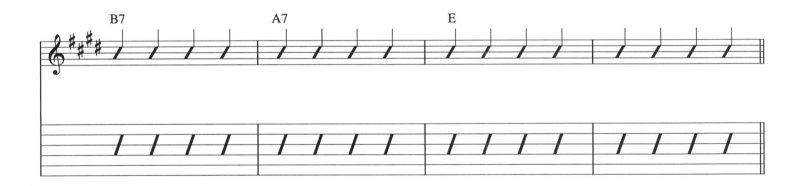

◆ Good Morning Blues

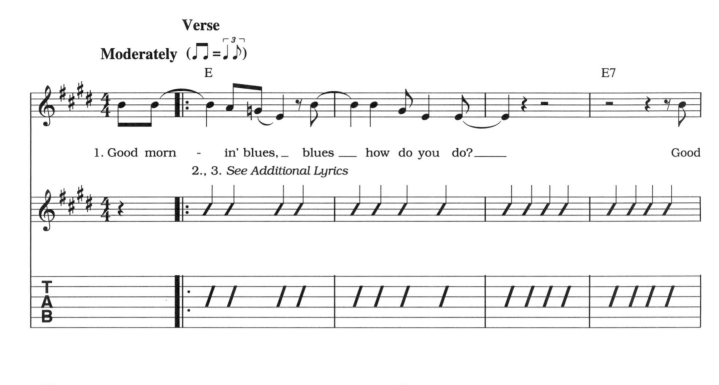

Verse

Moderately (♫ = ♩♪³)

1. Good morn - in' blues, __ blues __ how do you do? __

2., 3. *See Additional Lyrics*

Good

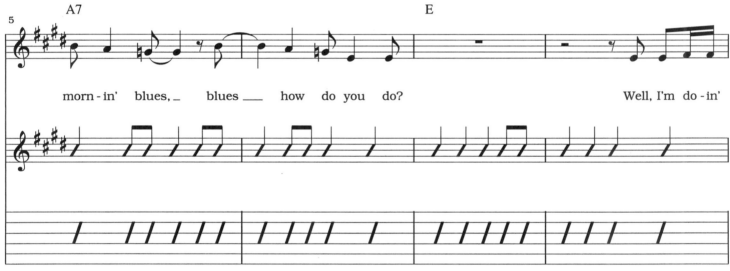

morn - in' blues, __ blues __ how do you do?

Well, I'm do - in'

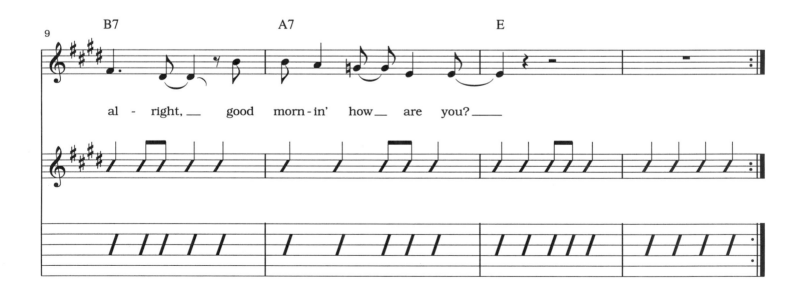

al - right, __ good morn - in' how __ are you? __

◆ 7 Turnarounds & Endings

Example 1 Turnaround

Insert at measure 11

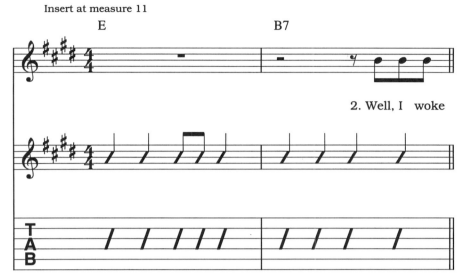

2. Well, I woke

Additional Lyrics

2. Well, I woke up this mornin',
   Blues all around my head.
   Woke up this mornin',
   Blues all around my bed.
   Went in to eat my breakfast,
   Blues was even in my bread.

Example 2 Common Blues Ending

Insert at measure 12

Example 3 Turnaround

Insert at measure 11

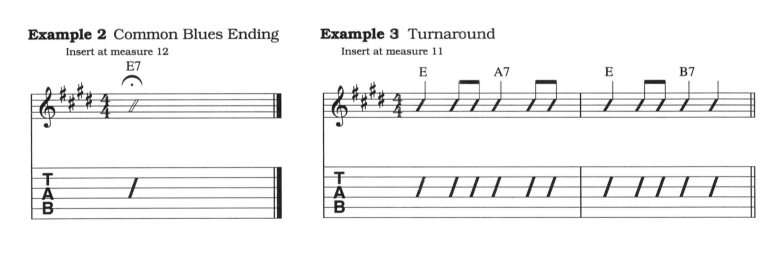

Additional Lyrics

3. I got blues in my coffee,
   Blues all in my tea.
   Got blues in my coffee,
   Blues all in my tea.
   I got blues in my family
   Between my wife and me.

Example 4 Turnaround

Insert at measure 11

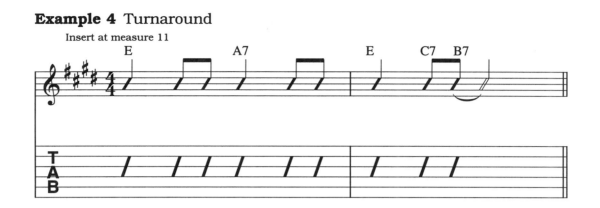

Example 5 Turnaround

Insert at measure 11

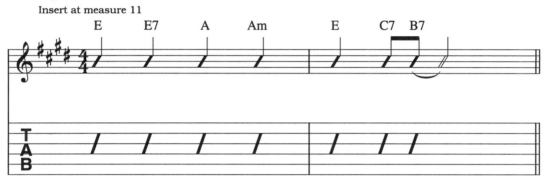

Example 6 Double-Stop Turnaround

Insert at measure 11

 **Fills**

Example 1

Insert at measure 3

Example 2

Insert at measure 3 and 7

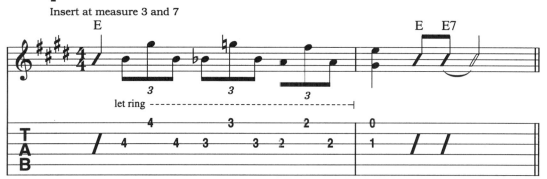

Example 3

Insert at measure 11

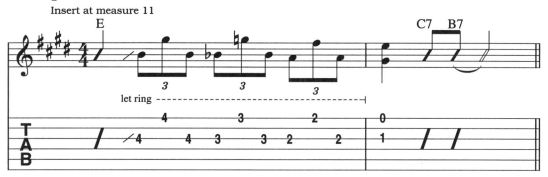

Example 4

Example 5

Example 6

⟨10⟩ Good Morning Blues

(with Fills)

Intro
Moderately (♪♪ = ♪♪)

E E7 A Am E C7 B7

Verse

E

4. I got the blues so bad __ that it hurts __

*P.M.   P.M.

*Palm Mute or damping.

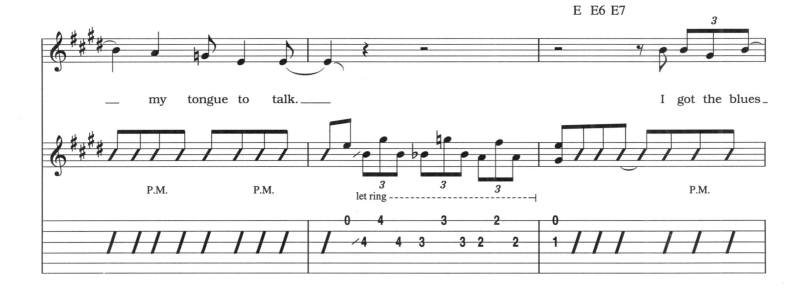

E E6 E7

__ my tongue to talk. __

I got the blues __

P.M.   P.M.   let ring ----------------------   P.M.

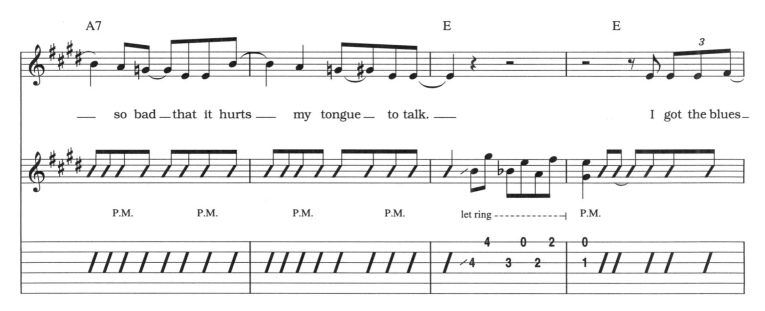

A7

E

E

__ so bad __ that it hurts __ my tongue __ to talk. __

I got the blues __

P.M.   P.M.   P.M.   P.M.   let ring ------------   P.M.

10

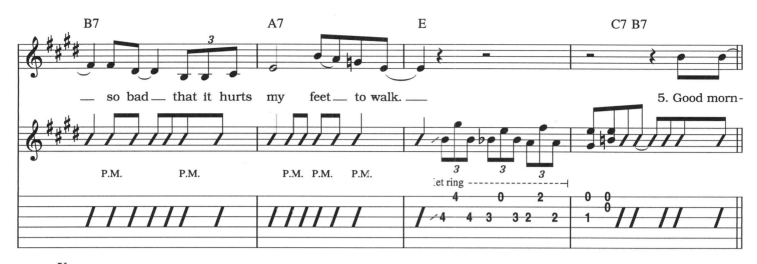

so bad — that it hurts my feet — to walk. —   5. Good morn-

Verse

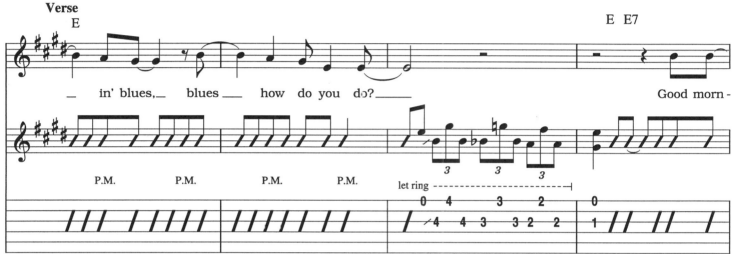

— in' blues, — blues — how do you do? —   Good morn -

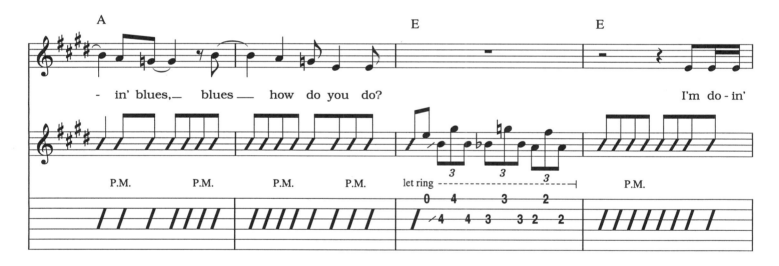

- in' blues, — blues — how do you do?   I'm do - in'

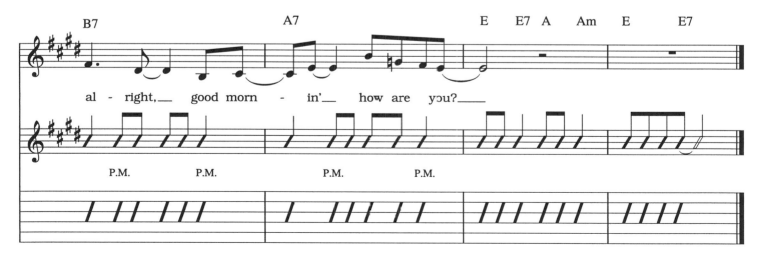

al - right, — good morn - in' — how are you? —

◆12 Rocking Bass Rhythms

Example 1

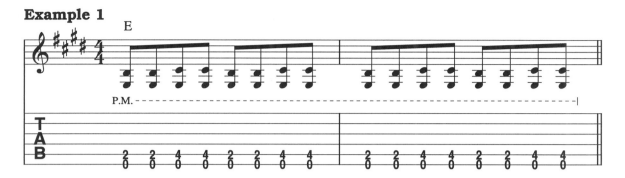

Example 2

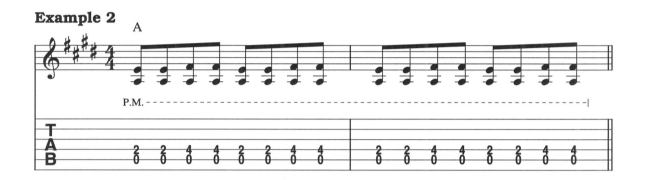

Example 3

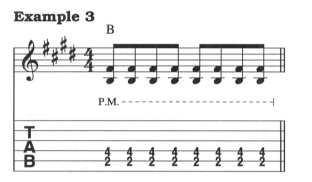

Example 4

Example 5

Example 6

Insert at measures 4 and 8

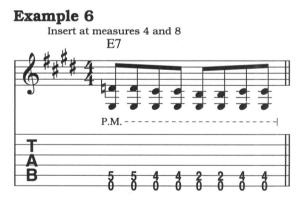

Example 7

Insert at measure 6

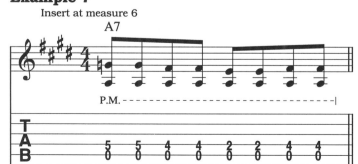

🔶14 Boogie Woogie Walking Bass

Moderately (♫ = ♩♪)

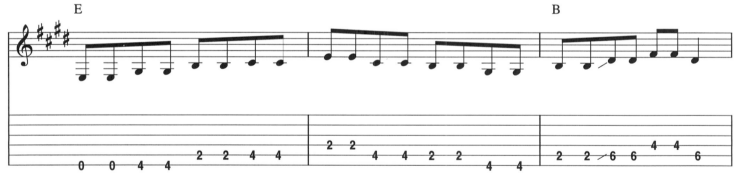

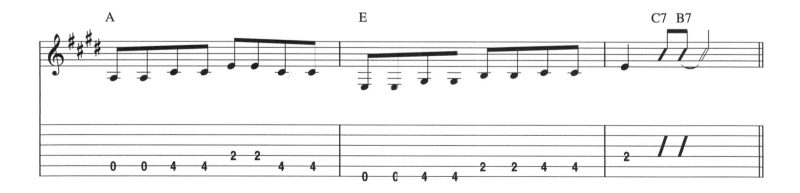

⟨15⟩ Bass Turnarounds

Example 1

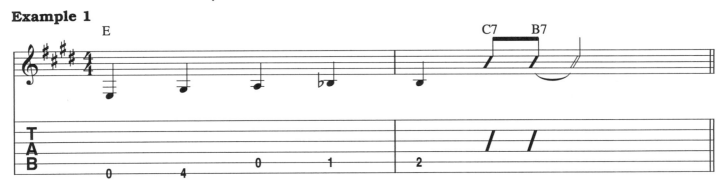

Example 2

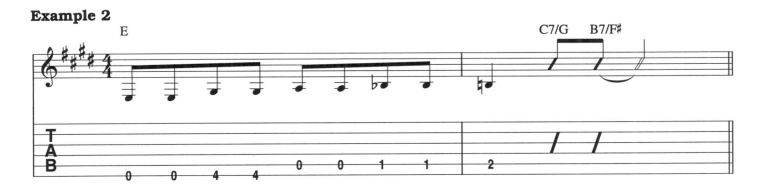

Example 3

Example 4 Happy's Favorite Turnaround   **Example 4**

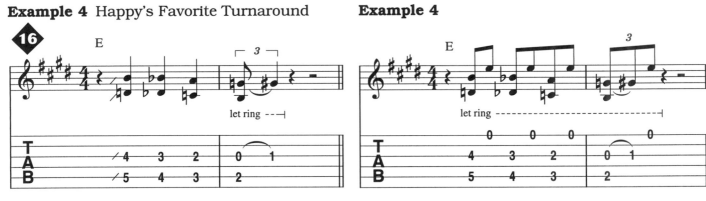

Example 6

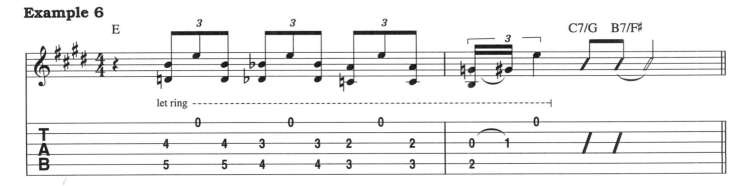

18 New Stranger Blues

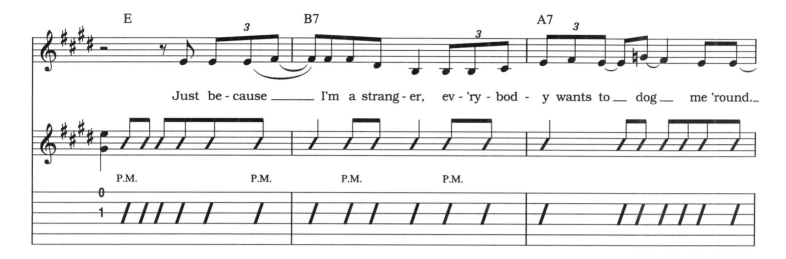

Just be-cause _____ I'm a strang-er, ev-'ry-bod-y wants to _ dog _ me 'round.

Verse

2. Lord, I won - der, do my good _____ gal know _ I'm here? _

I won-der, do my good gal know _ I'm here? _

Well, if _ she do, _ she sure don't _ seem _ to care. _

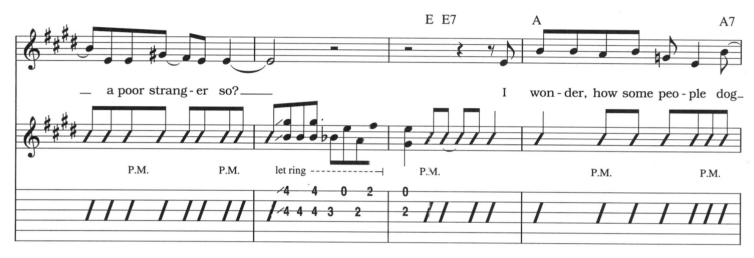

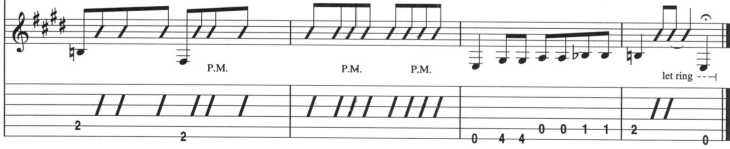

◆ 19 Fingerstyle Blues
Breaking Up the Chords

Example 1

Example 2

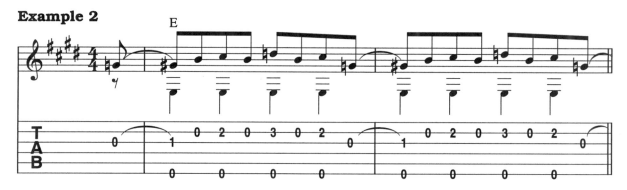

Example 3

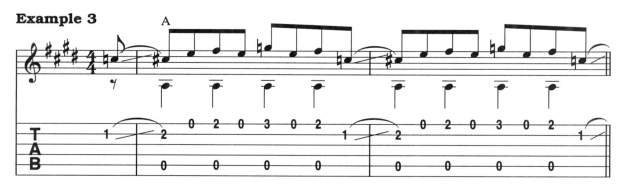

Example 4

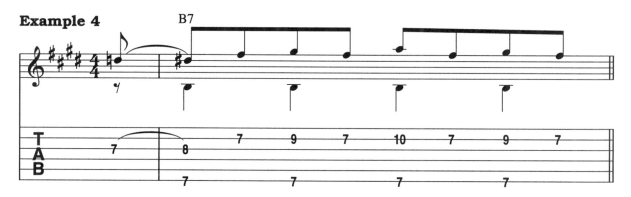

Example 5

◆20 Brownie's Lick

Moderately Fast (♫ = ♩♪³)

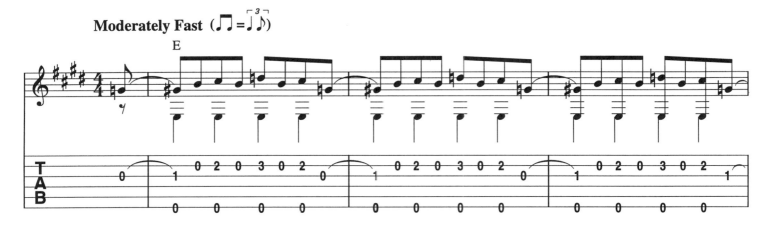

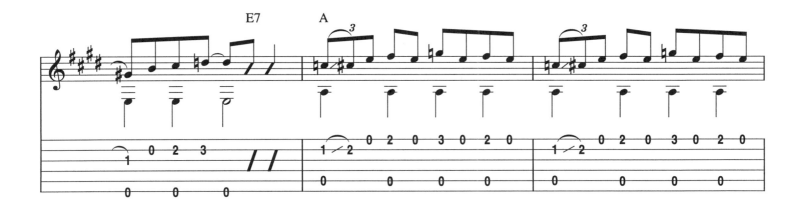

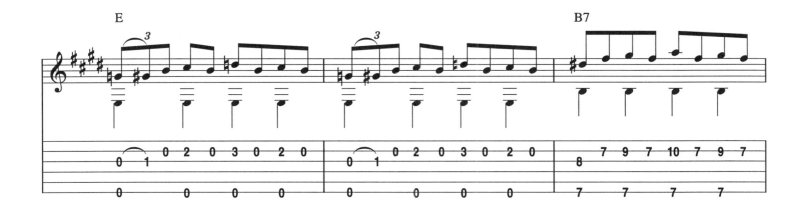

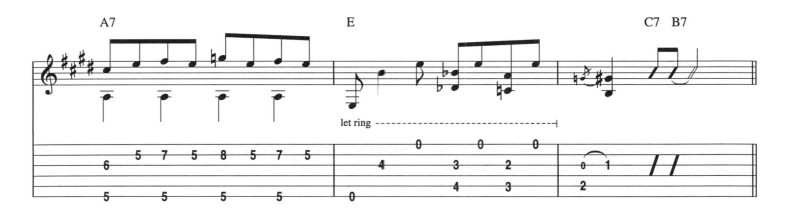

🔷22 Rock Me Mama

Intro
Moderate Slow Blues (♫ = ♩♪)

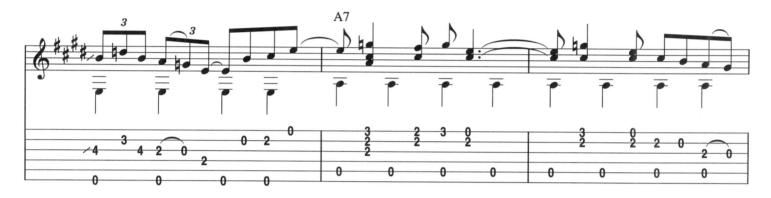

1. I said,—

Verse

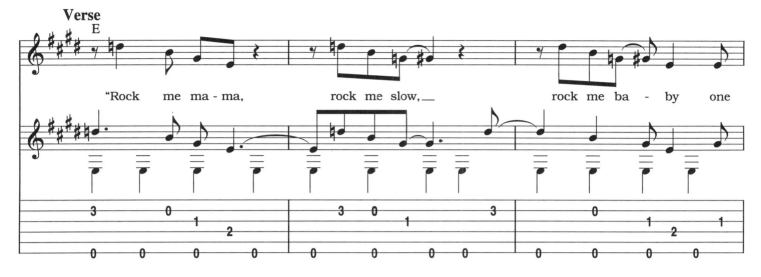

"Rock me ma - ma, rock me slow, rock me ba - by one

time be - fore you go." I said, "Rock me ma - ma, rock me all ___ night long."

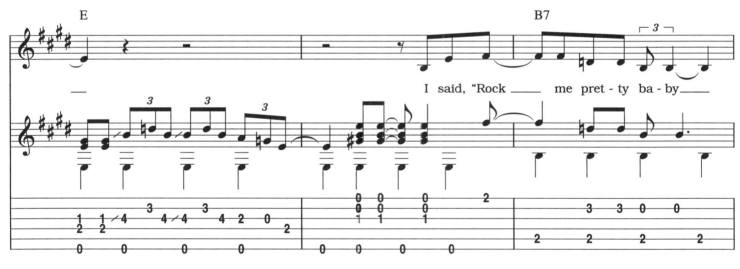

I said, "Rock ___ me pret - ty ba - by ___

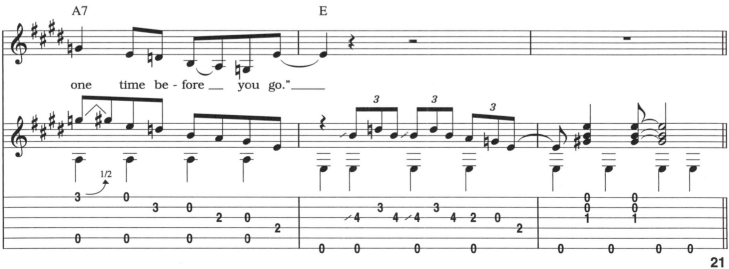

one time be - fore ___ you go." ___

Outro

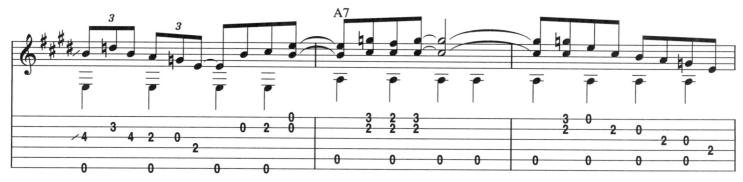

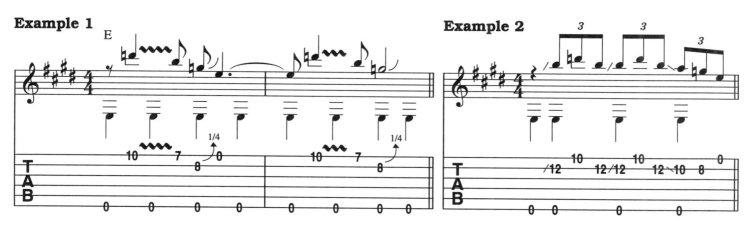

◆25 Octave Variations

Example 1

Example 2

27 In the Evening When the Sun Goes Down

Intro
Moderately Slow Blues (♪♪ = ♪³♪)

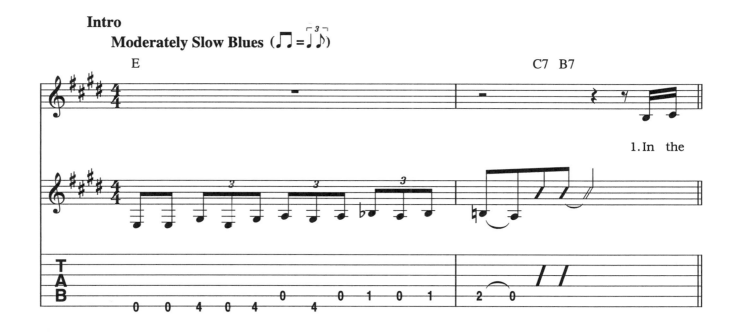

Verse

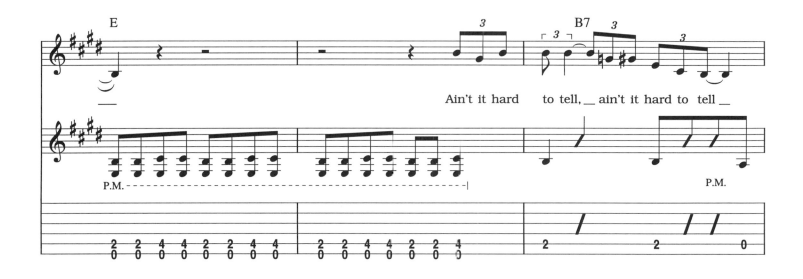

Ain't it hard   to tell, __ ain't it hard to tell __

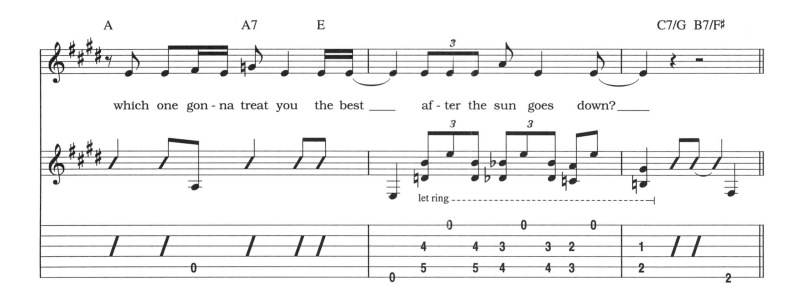

which one gon - na treat you   the best ____ af - ter the sun goes   down? ____

Guitar Solo

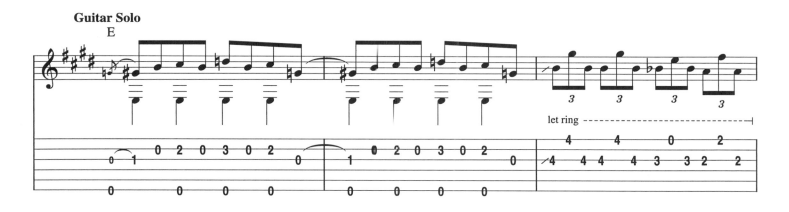

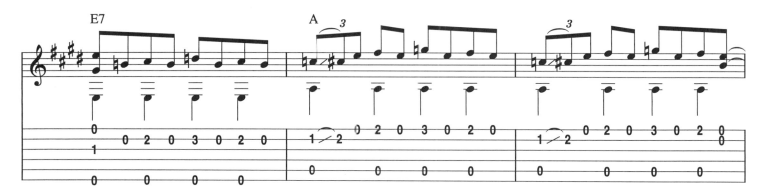

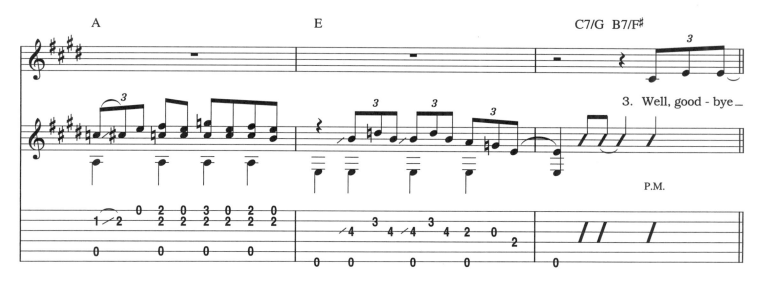

Verse

_ sweet-hearts and pals, _

you know I'll be go-in' a-way. _

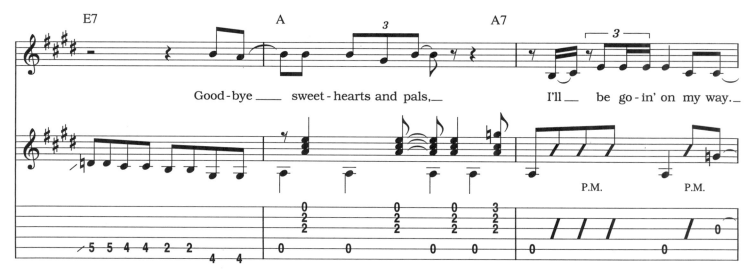

Good-bye _ sweet-hearts and pals,_

I'll _ be go-in' on my way._

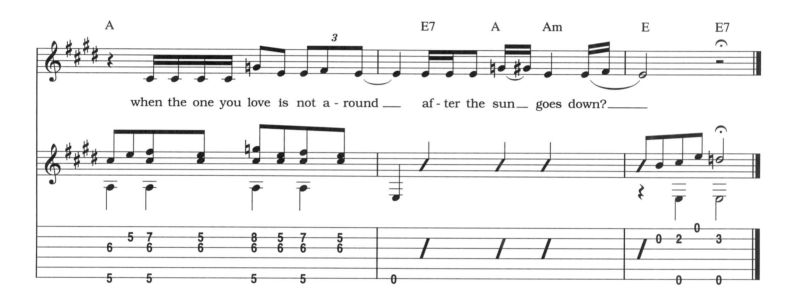

Chord Diagrams

 E

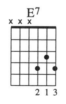 E7

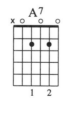 E7

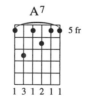 E6

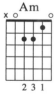 A

 A

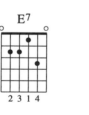 A7

 A7

 A7

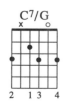 Am

B7

 B7

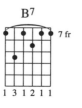 B7/F#

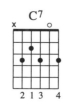 C7

C7/G

Biography

Happy Traum has been an active and important figure on the American music scene for nearly forty years. His avid interest in traditional and contemporary music has brought him recognition in many musical areas—as a performer, writer, editor, folklorist, teacher, and recording artist. A full-time musician since graduating from New York University in 1960, Happy has performed extensively throughout the U.S., Canada, Europe, Australia, and Japan, both as a soloist and as a member of various groups.

In 1958, while still a student at NYU, Happy started studying with blues guitarist Brownie McGhee, who became a big influence on his guitar style and technique. (Happy cites other guitarists as influences as well: Merle Travis, Mississippi John Hurt, Rev. Gary Davis and Lead Belly among them.) The two formed a long friendship that resulted in an instruction book called *The Guitar Styles of Brownie McGhee* (Oak Publications, 1971). Other books dealing with blues and other traditional guitar styles that Happy has written include *Fingerpicking Styles for Guitar, Contemporary and Traditional Fingerpicking Styles, The Blues Bag, Bluegrass Guitar, Flatpick County Guitar,* and *Folk Guitar as a Profession.*

Happy's intense musical involvement has been the driving force behind **Homespun Tapes**, the dynamic and growing music instruction company which Happy and his wife Jane founded in 1967. Since its inception he has personally produced approximately 400 music instruction lessons on audio cassettes and over 150 instructional video tapes, taught by top professional performing musicians.

A Selected Discography

With Various Groups:

Broadside (both solo and with The New World Singers) (with Bob Dylan, Phil Ochs, Pete Seeger, The Freedom Singers, and others)	1963	Folkways Records
The New World Singers (liner notes by Bob Dylan)	1964	Atlantic Records
The Children of Paradise	1966	Columbia (single)
Mud Acres: Music Among Friends	1972	Rounder (LP)
Woodstock Mountains: More Music from Mud Acres	1976	Rounder (LP)
Woodstock Mountains Revue: Pretty Lucky	1978	Rounder (LP)
Woodstock Mountains Revue: Back to Mud Acres	1981	Rounder (LP)
Woodstock Mountains: Music from Mud Acres (compilation)	1987	Rounder (CD)
Bring It On Home, Vol. 1 and 2	1994	Sony Legacy (CD)

With Artie Traum:

Happy and Artie Traum	1970	Capitol Records (LP)
Double Back	1971	Capitol Records (LP)
Hard Times in the Country	1974	Rounder Records (LP)
The Test of Time	1994	Roaring Stream Records (CD)

Solo:

Relax Your Mind	1975	Kicking Mule Records (LP)
American Stranger	1977	Kicking Mule Records (LP)
Bright Morning Stars	1979	Greenhays/Flying Fish (LP)
Friends and Neighbors	1983	Vest Pocket (cassette only)
Buckets of Songs	1988	Shanachie (CD)

With Others:

Bob Dylan's Greatest Hits, Vol. 2 (three songs)	1971	Columbia

HOMESPUN
LISTEN & LEARN SERIES
THIS EXCITING NEW SERIES FEATURES LESSONS FROM THE TOP PROS WITH IN-DEPTH CD INSTRUCTION AND THOROUGH ACCOMPANYING BOOKLET.

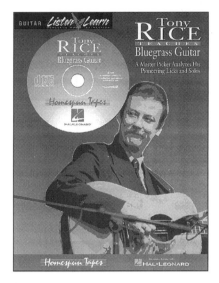

GUITAR

Tony Rice Teaches
Bluegrass Guitar*
A Master Picker Analyzes His Pioneering Licks And Solos

Tony Rice is known world-wide for his spectacular technique, brilliant improvisation and powerful soloing. In this lesson, he personally passes on to you the style he has developed during the two decades as the top bluegrass flatpicker of his generation. In careful detail, Tony analyzes licks, runs, solos and rhythm parts to hot bluegrass songs and fiddle tunes that will challenge and delight all flatpickers. Before long you'll be picking solos to the following essential bluegrass tunes: "The Red Haired Boy," "Little Sadie," "Your Love Is Like A Flower," "Blue Railroad Train," "Home From The Forest," "Wildwood Flower," "Old Train," "Wild Horse," and "Jerusalem's Ridge."

_____00695045 Book/CD Pack.....................$19.95

Happy Traum Teaches
Blues Guitar*
A Hands-On Beginner's Course In Acoustic Country Blues

Take a lesson in fingerstyle blues guitar from one of the world's most respected teacher/performers. All you need to know is how to play a few basic chords to get started playing along with this user-friendly book/audio package. Beginning with the most basic strumming of a 12-bar blues pattern, Happy gradually starts adding fills, runs, turnarounds, bass rhythms and "boogie woogie" walking bass patterns that make the basic blues progression come alive. All of these elements are notated in both notes and tab.

_____00841082 Book/CD Pack.....................$19.95

Richard Thompson Teaches
Traditional Guitar Instrumentals*
A Legendary Guitarist Teaches His Unique Arrangements To Irish, Scottish and English Tunes

Learn the techniques and style of traditional Irish, English and Scottish jigs, reels, hornpipes and other tunes arranged for fingerstyle guitar. On the CD, Richard explains how he uses altered tunings, string bends, vibrato as well as other techniques to give these tunes added "flavor." The book contains all of the songs and techniques written in notation and tab.

_____00841083 Book/CD Pack.....................$19.95

PIANO

David Cohen Teaches
Blues Piano
A Hands-On Beginner's Course In Traditional Blues

Sit down at the piano and start to boogie. This easy play along course will have you rockin' and rollin' in no time – even if you have never played blues piano before. David Cohen (The Blues Project, Country Joe and the Fish, etc.) starts you at the beginning, quickly getting you into the elementary theory needed to understand chord progressions and the 12-bar blues form. Then it's right into setting up a solid left-hand rhythm in the bass to create a bedrock for the right hand improvisations to come. By the time this lesson ends, you'll be jamming the blues, plus you'll have a solid foundation on which to build.

_____00841084 Book/CD Pack.....................$19.95

HARMONICA

John Sebastian Teaches
Blues Harmonica
A Complete Guide For Beginners

A rock 'n' roll legend teaches you everything you need to play great blues harp in this unique lesson. John Sebastian starts at the beginning, carefully explaining the proper way to hold the instrument and make your first tones. John explains and demonstrates essential techniques such as reed bending, vibrato, rhythm grooves, "cross harp" playing and more as well as several great blues licks and complete solos. Lessons are written in notation and tablature.

_____00841074 Book/CD Pack.....................$19.95

PENNYWHISTLE

Cathal McConnell Teaches
Irish Pennywhistle
A Hands-On Beginner's Course In Traditional Irish Repertoire And Technique

Learn to play traditional Irish songs on an instrument the whole family can enjoy. Cathal McConnell, known world-wide for his work with the popular Celtic band Boys of the Lough, teaches you the basics from the proper way to hold and blow the whistle, to the slurs, trills, rolls and other important techniques that will give you a truly Irish "feel." 12 traditional Irish folksongs are notated and explained in detail. As a bonus, the guitar accompaniment is recorded on one stereo channel while the pennywhistle is recorded on the other, so you can play along with only the accompaniment when you have mastered each tune.

_____00841081 Book/CD Pack.....................$19.95

FOR MORE INFORMATION, SEE YOUR LOCAL MUSIC DEALER, OR WRITE TO:

HAL•LEONARD™
CORPORATION
7777 W. BLUEMOUND RD. P.O. BOX 13819 MILWAUKEE, WI 53213

*Contains tablature